The Skin Diary

The Skin Diary

Abegail Morley

Nine
Arches
Press

The Skin Diary
Abegail Morley

ISBN: 978-1-911027-04-1

Copyright © Abegail Morley

Cover artwork © Eleanor Bennett
www.eleanorleonnebennett.com

All rights reserved. No part of this work may be reproduced, stored or transmitted in any form or by any means, graphic, electronic, recorded or mechanical, without the prior written permission of the publisher.

Abegail Morley has asserted her right under Section 77 of the Copyright, Designs and Patents Act 1988 to be identified as the author of this work.

First published June 2016 by:

Nine Arches Press
PO Box 6269
Rugby
CV21 9NL
United Kingdom

www.ninearchespress.com

Printed in Britain by:
The Russell Press Ltd.

Contents

Before you write off your imaginary sister	11
Summer	12
Nesting in the wardrobe	13
Childhood	14
Wrong name	15
Her story	16
Losing Elena	18
The Archive of Lost Lives	19
B1077	20
Bleeding	21
Taking flight	22
The winter gatherer	23
Discovery	24
The Blame	25
The shed = your secret life	26
If you stitch a woman	27
Neurologic Signature of Physical Pain	28
The Ice Hotel	29
Time Keeper	30
Brighton flat	31
Home	32
Still life with bathwater	33
The carrier bag	34
The Skin Diary	35
Back door at night	36
The Bramble Hotel	37
Pause	38
Love Child	39
The mechanics of loving	40
Last night	41
Summer's end in Hackney	42

Forgetting you	43
The Cabinet of Broken Hearts	44
Post-	45
Mayday	46
The swallowed self	47
The horologist and the body clock	48
Barefoot	49
Foundling	50
Counter turn	51
Chicken coop	52
Fertility spell	53
Achillea millefolium	54
Miracle	55
Fish wife	56
The Museum of Missed Opportunities	57
The Oncology Community	58
In the photo I never took	59
Paddock Wood to Charing Cross	60
Presence	61
text	62
After you've died	63
Afterwards in ink	64
After the funeral	65
Package	66
Living with bats	67
Jacket	68
Night planting	69
Acknowledgements	71

'As time goes on, you'll understand. What lasts, lasts; what doesn't, doesn't. Time solves most things. And what time can't solve, you have to solve yourself.'

Haruki Murakami

Before you write off your imaginary sister

remember how she didn't take her blunt playschool scissors
to your Tiny Tears doll, didn't lop off a curl,
how it didn't make you cry for three nights in a row,
your only consolation, not inviting a mantra to your lips:
You are not my sister, you are not my sister.

Think of that night she wasn't at the tap-end
of the bath, not blowing bubbles through her fingers,
not sloshing them over your face, how water didn't slop
over the bath's rim, how you didn't slip
when your mother hugged you out in a towel.

Memorise how she didn't cuddle close for those stories,
clap when they escaped the Gingerbread House. Learn how
she didn't travel with you on the school bus, wasn't there
when you rubbed your fingers over the invisible bruise
that couldn't yellow on your thigh, wasn't bashed by her bag.

Before you know it, she's not at your wedding,
taking the posy from your nervous hands, doesn't smile
when she doesn't do it. Bear in mind she didn't
have that look in her eyes when she didn't hold your son
in her arms in amazement. Learn by heart those miles

she couldn't take because you couldn't call her at two a.m.
thinking he might die from colic. Remember how
she doesn't say she loves you more now than ever, and how
desperate that cannot make you feel. And know now
all you can say is, *I miss you, I miss you.*

Summer

Corn scrapes our shins.
We've no reason to go back.
Now you're here, we spend summer
in fields far from our houses
where no-one can see.

We rub mud on naked arms;
put stripes across our faces,
blood-red clay over our noses,
tug back our hair.

We march by the river, sun scalds
our scalps, necks. From the back
I can tell you're not a boy;
your legs are too skinny, your
hips widening gently.

You flay corn with a slender
branch of willow – air whips round
your head faster, faster, you love
the noise. Sap spills in your palm.

We thrust our feet in water,
kick until we're soaked. Next thing
you're on the bridge, toes over its edge,
steadying yourself against the breeze.

You bend slightly, unlock your knees, leap.
You drop slowly through the air,
almost as if it's trying to catch you.

Nesting in the wardrobe

She takes her child-small fists from her pockets, shakes them
till her fingers tingle at the pads, shelters air in her palms
as if it were a white-blue egg that might just wake.

Her time ticks in shameful hours – cedared, Yardley-soaped,
she hides at the back behind black dresses, chiffon blouses,
knee-high boots until the lolling egg rolls from her grasp, blue-white,

slips from her fingertips and she watches it (as if in slow motion)
collide with the edge of the wardrobe door. Skull first,
struck like plate glass, she's stuck in no man's land

with only startled air and centimetres between them.
Her voice, huddled in her throat, lets out only the slightest sound,
amniotic fluid flows in rivulets down her wrists, spills like silk.

Childhood

She knows that sunrise grits its teeth,
spits wasps into daylight, sticks blind corners
on every street. She knows that the last time happens

over and over, that tears are for little girls
and what rhymes with *mad* are *sad* and *bad*.
This is her childhood strutting its stuff –

it never knew enough to get it right;
never knew why lemons weren't called yellows
or why a winter's night didn't seal her blood,

why gales never woke the dead. It didn't know
why, crouched in song, parcelled in blue bedding,
she smelled vanilla, chocolate, carefully cut her name

into the skirting knowing the moon already knew it by heart.
Her life is stored in a house of ruins
she's rebuilding brick by brick. If you visit tomorrow

she'll feed you fairy cakes on white china plates,
pour tea from an imagined pot.

Wrong name

When she tries to clamp her mouth around it,
the girl with the wrong name knows
it writhes like sheep caught on wire,

remembers rigid hidden vowels,
consonants scratching like lichen in her throat.
She clears it – a scorched earthy sound

resonates in vocal chords, sways this way
and that, until it settles unthreaded.
For the first twelve years, if someone asked

her name she'd lay it flat on her tongue
until it uncurled stiffly, like cloth in ice,
stayed on its tip, a left-behind phrase,

an old-fashioned term yearning to release itself.
But in her tiny doll-house world
she rams in her thumb so it can't escape.

Her story

I.

Inside where darkness stops,
her bones are soft, pliable, head

half her weight. She curls in the curve
of a crescent moon. Week 28,

she feels pain. Inhales, exhales;
downy hairs hem her skin, like his.

Waters break.

II.

Her room's changed shape, dimension.
No longer measured crown to rump,

she stretches her length, cranks up
Amy Winehouse, reads *To the Lighthouse*

in her bed at night. She meets pain.
Inhales, exhales; dyes her hair, like his.

Opens *The Waves.*

III.

Outside, morning blisters. I feel
her shift. Away. Resist.

She submerges, airless. Week 936,
head full of dreams half her weight

she buckles under, greets pain.
Inhales, exhales. Her hair skims

the water's skin.

Losing Elena

When I was eight I made a pact with my invisible friend
that our friendship wouldn't end when we grew up.

At eighteen we lacked the confidence to part, so I took her
to read English at Hull, shoved her invisible things

in a corner of my room, clutched them close at night –
they smelt of nutmeg, warm milk, coddled eggs.

I knew all her tricks by then – moving stuff at midnight
as if wind sucked the room's air till its ribs collapsed,

lifting clothes like a tornado had skimmed the room.
In the canteen she'd steal reflections from spoons,

take bites of my food, sip coke till bubbles
went up her nose. She'd pose in shop mirrors, hang

around their windows, walk in time with me down
roads. She began to weigh stone-heavy. One night

we played cards, winner disappears. It was late,
we'd drunk too much in the Union bar.

At three that morning I opened the door, felt
the street's sharp draught meet her, sweep her away.

Sometimes I phone her up for a chat, but a shriek sticks
to the back of my throat as if it has nowhere else to go.

The Archive of Lost Lives

Halfway in it catches you, scrapes the back
of your larynx. Acid-free boxes in neat rows
cram shelves, catalogued in date order,

packed with could-bes cracking like vertebrae –
an ash-womb fossilised by time. With steady
gloved hands untie the knot of unbleached cotton

that circles pages, let a ghost-life rise like brick dust.
See stained fingers of childhood, no longer
mitten-warm, map worlds on sugar paper,

the promised love of later life marble-white, except
for tiny red veins like hair, tulle or the mesh of nets
like those she used to hook butterflies.

All she caught were shadows on garden walls,
colds in the depths of winter, chicken pox at
primary school, verrucas at swimming pools,

the tide on East Looe Beach that bumped her
two miles down the coast. Goose-skinned when they
found her, lungs slaked with brackish water.

B1077

We spent that afternoon at a watermill outside Easton,
watched it turn for a time, then willed it to stop –
noticed how trees had tipped their branches
leftwards as if to let wind through.

It happened in Cookley. Your voice on the phone
untangles down the line. I think of an asthma attack,
a hospital, but that isn't it you say. You insist
it's a collision on a B road, her 4x4 hit head on,

how a woman had stopped, held her.
At the funeral three weeks from now her mother
will tell me there wasn't a mark on her,
how she looked like Princess Diana. But now

I don't know that, just know your voice journeys
through wires to reach me, stutters along
overhead cables as if you control the skies, the birds,
the welcome rain that clears the air.

Bleeding

I.

When you text to say you'll bring a radiator key,
suddenly you're my knight in shining armour –

you can conquer lands, slay dragons
with your sword. And I fall in love with your words,

the *Yes, I have one*, the *I'll put it in my bag*.
Here is my hero at the end of a phone

texting all the wooing words a girl needs,
now it's winter, snowing outside.

II.

When you left, the radiator still needed bleeding,
air locked between pipes and room:

a word, a sentence, a message.
I listened to the gasp

when I turned the key,
but couldn't quite hear what you said.

Taking flight

In the lazy twilight he snaps his hand over
his mouth as if stemming his last words,
as if saying them will somehow draw water
from the moat, slime from a stone, bottles from

the bed, fish from their spot beneath weed.
He stiffens as bats whistle past our heads,
forms a perfect frown when they settle in arched
windows, wings taut, frail bodies back-lit

by the moon, hearts thumping in unison.
We lean into a wall, muffle our mouths so they
don't know we're here, listen to the slap, slap
of water on bank until we gulp down air –

our ribcages heave, give us away; two birds
clap their wings, head off across the quarry, startled.
When the moat isn't expecting it, he skims a stone
across its surface, taking it by surprise.

The winter gatherer

Today you say life with me
is winter, but it's all there is.

Here, untouched, I ache;
cold parcels my bones,

ties me tight with ice-stiff string.
You've forgotten how it was,

your eyes now snow-blinded –
sun on ice can do that.

Wind whips in from the east,
slams my spine. My lungs hang empty.

In front of my mouth steam freezes –
my last words are *hoar, frost.*

Discovery

I think it must be hidden, something dead behind
the mower, tucked in a corner – a skull
or a flapless wing. He clenches my wrist,

his body says, *Move, move.* I edge forward to
where sky has drawn a line on the wooden floor,
screeched through a gap that runs the length of the roof,

casting its own sunset. I trip through its rays, his hand
still on mine – iron-gripped. He shifts ahead,
tip-toeing like a child in a game of Big Bad Wolf.

This is the house he built, not of straw, but guts, blood,
sweat. At the back, in the dark, hauled up under matting
and compost, a cat and her kittens watch us kneel,

crawl ever so slowly towards their terrified eyes.
If I could, I'd wrench words from myself, curve them
in the light that outlines their bodies, tell them

not to inhale too deeply, not to get a taste for life.

The Blame

I wish I'd kept evidence in matchboxes, jam jars stopped
with cotton wool, documented it on sapless leaves,
their spines bent back to sudden silence. I don't know

if baling up your hair in envelopes and posting
through incurious letterboxes makes things easier.
Perhaps I should trace your face on carbon paper,

let it ache blue from the page, ask people if they really think
you did it. My smallest thought now loops back on itself,
gifts old ghosts to undim themselves, flounder

in the unlit house. Tonight I hear you stumble up steps,
four years after. Short shadows on brickwork thicken –
if I was prone to fancy, I would imagine you here.

The shed = your secret life

You repeat yourself as if some kind of vow
is wedged in your teeth, a small sad door

you're trying to leave by, its hinges straying
with the wind, metal on creaking wood.

You calculate how many times you might want
to come and go, rub creosote on your sleeve,

side-step a smell of paint stiffening its frame.
Sheds are for nails, blades;

you have a need for both, telling me this
through the moth-eaten space of your mouth.

Words now tumbleweed, but somehow
I've lost the gist, focused too closely on your lips

which are held in place as if stitched on
by someone who can't sew.

If you stitch a woman

from inside out there are no frayed edges
where you cut the seams, no threads pulled,
twisted or knotted. Armholes don't whimper
at being drawn too tight.

Fasten the collar in the secret knowledge
you can coil it, ruffle it, put a hook and eye
through it, make a river of herringbone.
You can saddle stitch, satin stitch, suffocate

with blanket stitch, hurry through
journeys, holding it up to the sky.
Watch her weaving, warp and webbing,
pin eyelets, embroider her mind so she sees

pictures of empty streets, sleeps in your cotton
sheets, wakes with your head on her hemline.
Use a rotary cutter to slice her into strips,
interline and interlock like she's your lover,

like they are your children. Stuff her lungs
with kapok, feathers, fibre, they will still
breathe on their own. You can make a red crêpe
heart that really beats, use safety pins that sing

through skin, plait ribbons of water to drip from
her eyes, pucker her lips so they stay silent, patch up
her mouth so it can't say she wants the length of her
unpicking, unbinding – just for one night.

Neurologic Signature of Physical Pain

Functional magnetic resonance imaging (fMRI): recent neuroscientific evidence suggests that empathy for pain activates similar neural representations as the first-hand experience of pain
  – C. Lamm et al, PLoS, (2007).

They say there is a theory for pain,
a mathematical formula –
it's not a threshold issue
it is to do with pain itself,
not its effect. If you look

through an electron microscope
you can see it huddled
in one corner of the slide,
a sticky mass of grey cells.
Under magnification

you can see a woman
with a black eye, keeled over,
her left leg slightly out of focus.
In front is a child, her hands
over her face – if you pan in

you can see the moons
of her nails, each of her tears.
Of course, you need
a control group – some pain
is more intense than others.

There needs to be a level
playing field; it's best
observed over time. She
does not have time.

The Ice Hotel

In the Ice Hotel there are no doors,
just air gapping between walls.
Outside in our thermals,
we watch the Northern Lights,
point up at the night sky
like we're children waiting for Santa.
I'm wearing a too-tight hat made from rabbit
and can't hear what you're saying.
I'm wondering if this is how it feels
to be sucked into a black hole.

*

You tell me there's a plant called Hawksbeard
that shuts its head three hours after pollination,
then mouth the words *I love you*, as if underwater,
or behind glass. I think of flower heads locking down
as soon as it's dusk, rocking inward like a skull.
Blue lights flash on your face. Outside, on the
street, a woman has closed herself into a ball
and paramedics are trying to help.
It's no good, I say, mouthing through glass.
It's too dark, it's too dark.

*

I'm watching the Northern Lights,
remembering that item on the news
about a woman with locked-in syndrome,
wonder if she can see hospital lights
flicking through her clamped-down lids.
Or if she can see the blackness of her heart,
or pale red of her blood as it lugs
itself around her body, or her neurons
bursting like fireworks just beneath her skin.

Time Keeper

I said everything I could before you stopped me,
sifted skin through hourglass after hourglass –

unshut my body till it tipped, arms flipped open,
hands skidding dough-white down panes. I know

the emptiness of hands, yet lift them to you, show
how my invisibility shimmers down glass, let you

pick me out, unsuspecting, from a line of women.
I know the dull heaviness of the bulb, struggle

at the timer's neck, my present somewhere between past
and future. There's a glimmer of me someplace, I'm sure.

Brighton flat

Our story is that of heaped book shelves,
a sultry summer's afternoon in that Brighton flat,
where even two flights up sand has trapped
itself in the stairwell, glistening frostlike

as we pass. We're holding a bag between us,
it sags heavy with the weight of potatoes,
a newspaper hanging from its top – a forlorn
seagull tapping against my leg as I struggle up

each step. I've learnt not to be scared of the dog
on the ground floor, but not yet its owner,
whose handprints on the glass fit mine,
perfectly. You laughed when I told you. Today

I decide not to touch anything, waddle against
the wall, ignore the wooden handrail,
barking dog, sand billowing across the hall.
On the way back from the shops, sun shimmered

on a lost hub-cap in the gutter; I felt the ache
of its metal against tarmac, the loss of its wheel.
Tonight you tell me, in a voice you've never owned,
that people, like sand, can become stranded forever.

Home

Everything stays as you left it –
leak sputtering in the bathroom,

square hole above the kitchen sink,
coving shoved in a corner.

I know drops in the bucket are you,
the way they swallow so much space.

It's bitter, pipes rattle,
clatter under floorboards.

Rain scuds in from the west,
our room is raw; clogged with ice.

The sheets under my weight
remain chilled in the night

like an absence, like they're not mine.

Still life with bathwater

He went after changing a washer in the tap,
left a wrench on the side of the bath,
a knot of blackness in his belly, a darkness
in his head. Instead of sitting alone
I twist both taps, gingerly at first
so they squeeze water like blood from stone.
Then, when I know it's just me and the night,
I push them wide, water splaying
like white swan wings striding the bath,
splurging over its edge, onto the mat.
I know he's not coming back. He took
a bag full of things, shirts, socks, sacrifices –
he said he made a lot of those. Earlier, I'd watched
them wave like flags as he tugged his case away.

The carrier bag

I empty myself like quicksilver, pour
an ankle-deep pool on the kitchen floor,
take up two seats on the bus –
one for me and one for the pool.

I call it *Heartbreak*, carry it with me,
sometimes in a Waitrose bag, latterly
in one from Aldi; it's firmer,
contains the liquid better.

I take it to a church in Holt,
have it blessed by the priest, show
it to a window cleaner outside M&S,
raise it aloft to the waves

at Holkham Beach so they get a good view.
At home, by an electric fire, I watch
it steam, mist the windows, write
Heartbreak was here – then wait

until all the bulges in the bag
turn in on themselves, collapse.
Heartbreak was here dries slowly.
Disappears.

The Skin Diary

Because I pack everything, there's no room
for it to hide its hurt in the pockets of my case.
There's no place to scar its roots, no roots
to put down in this town, or the next, or the next.

This skin flinches at four a.m. when I heave it
to the car, let headlights rip along stitches
it might have had if I knew a way to make
it whole. This stretch of skin loses itself

to things it's felt, traps them below
downy hairs, tangles its dreams in a web
of veins it's carried all its life, never let go.
It smells of muffins, cigarettes, regret

of that bottle of wine the day before. This skin
can't sing out of doors, can't bear another night
tightly blanketing these bones. It's paper thin;
days roadmap its waxen wrists.

It wonders what to do now night has ended,
how to fend for itself without my body's ticking.
I announce the miracle of absence,
leave it outside the front door, tell it to wait

for my return, reverse out the drive. I wonder
if it will raise up its hands to pray or wave.

Back door at night

Three steps down and I'm out in the garden.
A hunched moon picks its way through trees, hangs low

like a goose's abdomen, almost touches the ground. I tiptoe
over slabs, cold in my short sleeves, pyjama bottoms trailing

through damp grass. Above me nothing save the night sky, drifting.
If there were owls they'd echo across fields,

badgers would scatter earth, scutter through thickets,
snag pelts on twigs, scent the air.

But there's just me, a door key, a moss-grown path
and a desire to crawl into my own cul-de-sac.

The Bramble Hotel

I know when it's time. Everything's
too loud – the kettle hisses, clicks on and off,
washing machine moans in the corner,

doorbell buzzes, razor-sharp without easing;
the whole house jangles for no reason.
When it's time to check-in, I go to the garden,

heave my body through unmanaged branches
that root from the tip of each node,
struggle past leaves, mottled, flaxen.

The ticking in my head revs up a gear,
synapses zip like fireflies; ordinary people
say they grow from glow-worms,

abdomens red, yellow, green.
They feed on shit; I know they're beetles,
crepuscular, nothing but bugs.

In the Bramble Hotel there's no luminescence,
just criss-crossing, a dot-to-dot drawing
in red ink, linking one cut to another

as thorns rake skin. I am their victim;
I am sin. In my en suite I bathe in jelly,
smear *Rubus fructicosus* over each shoulder,

sink back in a froth of wild fruit, let drupelets
hang down my spine: wait
for rotting crop, larvae, vinegar flies.

Pause

So he told me that by speaking fast
his sadness couldn't catch him –
he'd leave it behind on some highway,
its pulse quickening on the verge,
but an urge to carry on wouldn't leave him.

He kept running up streets,
lights at crossings blinking amber,
mouth wordlessly moving
up and down and from a distance
it looked like he was saying, *Because, because.*

I checked the back of his head,
watched the yank of his neck
pull itself into a brisk arc –
it was like he was dying at high speed,
his mouth too hungry for words.

And when a part of me let him go,
he slowed down, a stitch
in his side calmed to an incantation.
He dropped his hand into mine.
I wanted to say, *Because, because.* But couldn't.

Love Child

I store the potato, peeled, covered in polythene.
When I open the fridge the motion of the door rocks it
to and fro like a skull. Tonight on my way home,
I nod to the grocer who, drenched in electric light,

sprouts wings like Phanes. His hands are grubby, old.
I wonder how they'd feel on my body, what he'd say
about the empty fruit bowl, how he'd bend to kiss
the top of my head while checking my kitchen:

cafetière, wine, bread. I know in the morning
those fingers will plunge down coffee
and I'll smell it here at the top of the house, hope
he doesn't take milk, pray he doesn't open the fridge;

I know he'll fan out his fat hands, hold the hollows
of the fontanelles, cradle it like a baby's head.

Mechanics of loving

Notice how my name is not so sure
anymore – blood thin,
a framework of flesh.
My breath calls to his,
moth-like, tapping glass.

I feel the sleepless hypnotism
of his heart thumping,
waves on the hull
of a ship lost in fog.

Last Night

The rain is all but gone – I can't tell
if it's the trees dripping now.
I push my hand upwards as if to catch
a drop, but really I'm looking

at a lit window three flights up
where you're drizzling oil into a hot pan,
a glass of Merlot poured, a cheap
candle, slightly too white,

sputtering from the table. I stand
in this much-loved place, in the view,
our view, the one that made us
buy this house. I'm part of the street

we strolled down at night to make sure
it was safe, drove past at rush hour
to check traffic, ambulances, road rage.
But there's a silence tonight,

so quiet I can hear myself walking
up those three flights, an end-of-day
weary tread, the kind that makes you think
your lungs won't inflate, your knees

can't bear your weight. In your wallet
I know there's a photo of me
taken at Salthouse last summer –
I know you creased it slotting it in

under the plastic, cursed yourself
as you did it. I know other things too,
but I'll save them with the rain I can feel
in my palm as I wait to feel you.

Summer's End in Hackney

So that she might go unnoticed, she doesn't turn on
the sitting-room light when street lights gutter,

announce evening in a sudden gust of white
that catches out the rain. She wonders if it's okay

to start drinking at four, winter nights creep in
ever earlier. In the kitchen she greets the fridge:

they blink at each other for a minute –
she reaches for wine, grabs like it's ripe on the vine,

the Veneto sun freckling her arms, a 50 kilo basket
dragging her backwards into hot earth.

She presses the bottle to her cheek, remembers how
each grape was too low to squat for, too low not to stoop –

how she spent that holiday, spread the full-length
of his bed watching first light distil the dawn,

splash through shutters, ooze across the room.

Forgetting you

When silence stops scribbling on emulsioned walls,
winds no longer threaten the letterbox, wolflike,
and streets haven't spent half the night watching

for your return, I'll roll over. One night I might sleep –
imagine myself tipping back and forth on a wooden swing
in winter, rope rubbing branch. But this morning I lie awake

you're still unvanished, unravelled in my temporal lobe –
a petal, or foetus. I unsing you from my world,
struggle to remove the earworm that constantly whines.

The Cabinet of Broken Hearts

Some still beat, shocked by their removal,
attached to the memory of their bodies.

Others stop the fight early on like newborns
losing life, lodestones stripped of magnetism.

They feel the agony of their ghosts leaving like dust
from snapped-shut attic trunks, weightless

as first light. Hearts don't understand death, think
of tissue, the rhythmical song of blood,

long to squat in the predictable warmth
of a rib's cave. Unwrapped, laid out

they resemble withered peaches, cracked
wintered stones, crows' heads rotting on roads.

They've forgotten how to pump, flex muscle,
dedicate their lives to someone else.

Post-

This package is securely wrapped.
I'm eating buttered toast surveying
its string, Sellotape, a date blurred
in the top right corner.

It circled Queen's Square at least four times
before you dropped it in a postbox,
let it fall from your grip, two hands, one hand,
gone. You probably took a detour

at the Coach and Horses, Dutch courage,
so somewhere between windmills
and drop dead drunk you'd tossed it,
along with your broken heart

(you tell me this later) into the first
postbox you saw. So now, when I open it
you're here next to me, astonished
that it's arrived today

when you've changed your mind
about leaving. I cut the string, you wince.
I tip out the contents, let them curve
in my bowl-shaped palm.

You say you hate inflicting pain.
Somehow I don't believe you.

Mayday

In the dull copper morning after he left,
her life pauses – a thought flees
mid-sentence, breath blurs between her lips –
a ship inching home through brume.

She takes her breakfast outside
to a small forbidden patch of sun
that keels over from next door, spreads itself
on her patio like a nylon spinnaker.

When she feels she's going under she returns,
throws dishes in the sink, trails the house seams
for clean clothes, brushed hair, broad shoulders –
finds shaving foam, a blunt razor spattered

with bristles. She mouths the word *drowned*,
rinses blades under the tap –
he dissolves – leaves without ceremony,
a deep sea fishing boat slipping harbour.

The swallowed self

This morning I wake to find a smaller me
burrowed in my lung cavity, setting up shop,
touting her wares. I smell freshly squeezed

limes, unmeasured, over-spiced curry;
ginger sliced in wide strips. I prefer herbs:
rosemary, flat-leafed parsley, coriander.

When I'm fast asleep she frazzles bacon –
the next day I fill my shopping basket
with smoked streaky. Now she's taken up knitting

which makes me cough clouds of knots,
knit-one-pearl-one, a hurl of needles tat-tat-tatting.
I rattle inside. When she starts stitching bridal gowns,

chooses fabrics, lace, a nice bolt of chiffon,
I'll sell myself online, marry the first man
who clicks my profile, likes my status.

The horologist and the body clock

I give him this mechanical body –
a skeleton case he can peer through,
lay my inner workings bare: the shape
of my spleen, contours of my liver,

my clay-heavy kidneys. I let him uproot
the spinal cord so its springs stutter,
begin recording the passage of time.
He listens to the tick-tock of my heart

through the locked-in glass, sees
a balance-wheel oscillate more calmly
depending on how close he comes.
I'm not shy when he looks at my ovaries,

pale pebbles beached in the womb,
or watches eggs like unstrung beads queue
at the top of fallopian tubes, make
their own slow journey through time.

Barefoot

I step from the bed, from a sea of children
twisting in cotton, bread for the trail
smuggled in their ample pockets, hands

over their eyes so they can't be seen. I see them
still their bodies. My blood spills,
comes back each month, merges sky with tide,

and my child's face, her birthplace beyond the shoreline,
dips behind each wave. I bring up the top sheet,
tuck it round her cheeks, rest a kiss on her forehead.

The sea swells, my feet sink deeper.

Foundling

We find her shoes under the hearth
matted with London clay, straw –
you saw where they'd walled up
a cat, but didn't tell me for years.

When the door shuts I know it's her,
put out Madeira cake, biscuits, sweets
on a plate smaller than my fist, push it
to the table's edge so she can reach.

I hold the bruised leather shoes,
brown laces – feel a soft foot in each,
their warmth on my fingers. I stow them
in the bedside table and after you turn out

the light, pull them under the duvet,
draw her body to mine. She smells
of apples, earth, hay; her hands, purple
from picking berries, knit into mine.

By morning she's gone. I hear you throw
away her food, crash her plate in the
dishwasher. I think of the cat, the tiny
shoes, and what it is we're burying now.

Counter turn

Every month it happens, slides down glass like rain,
the pain of it re-arranges itself like a thought passing
in the shape of you – an ancient language muttering,

running out of time, sand-heavy in the timer.
I can tilt it back up; let it glide down again,
its colour a litany of lost libraries

eking grain by grain. A hundred years later
we'll skate on the lake of lost children, ride on the bones
of their home-grown bodies, accidently fall into their arms.

Chicken coop

I gather up the chickens
as best as I can,
boots stuck in mud, shit,

westerly billowing my jacket.
It howls round my hood.
I herd them up the plank,

precocious Anconas, Faverolles,
wrench down the sliding bolts,
press them to their perches.

Wait for eggs.

Fertility spell

Your voice is shallow, hard
to decipher – in here I'm as blind
as a sack full of starlings.

Hessian-trapped I thrash,
a mass of wings and feathers,
stark eyes black as currants

glint, prick the dark,
eyelids flash scissor-like,
beak yellow as yolk.

My eggs ripening like waxy lemons.

Achillea millefolium
for luck

She has 800 chances of fertilisation –
scatters a packet of yarrow seeds

in a rake-prepared bed at the top
of the garden. Yesterday she dug deeply,

weeded, filled watering-cans
from a rain-drenched butt, fed the soil

until it was cool, moist. She knows
about staking, training, self-sowing.

In a yellow hospital lab half-way across
town her harvested eggs are stripped

of their outer cells, put into a Petri dish,
prepared for germination.

Miracle

Even now, with only a salt craving,
I taste you as if you're the sea under
its membrane when it's impossible

to tell surf from wave. You're the thinness
that laps shorelines at night when oceans
hanker after dunes, barge up beaches

like cargo trundling on rails. For ten years
you've lain dormant, a chest
jewel-ridden at the bottom of the sea.

Now you rise, accumulate in its froth,
piggy-backing on the tide. You've nested
in the earth's bowl, a whim of memory

sinking into sand. You've choked our past
in the current's path, pooled it in the Atlantic –
it drifts in the turn of light, empty, forgiving.

Fish wife

The woman who's not my mother has wave-wrinkled skin,
fingers red from filleting fish, dragging knives along their backs,
scales sticking like stars. Her thumbs are snagged by bones,
broken ends of warp, the pulp of her fingers painful, swollen.

The woman who's not my mother doesn't quail when she cuts off
the head, doesn't flinch as she detaches the stomach, doesn't blink
at the yield of flesh that slithers on plates. She prises open clams
with ease, rinses her oyster-shucker's hands in harsh water.

The woman who's not my mother dries them down her apron;
the start of a song trembles on her lips – a secret yearning
twists in her belly, shifts like a shoal of fish skimming
the water's surface, tails shimmying in sunlight.

The Museum of Missed Opportunities

They rest under glass, limp on unbleached muslin,
carefully placed by a white-gloved curator who
plucked them from my life as if pick-pocketing time.

He laid them out – unwrapped promises, wrens' eggs
freed from cotton wool, the shape of water from cool
mountain streams. Displayed, they suffocate under

the creak of onlookers who lean their full weight
on the cabinets, press fingers above pieces,
leave their own blurred history in its print –

tick items off catalogues, scrunch their eyes tight
as if squinting out the sun. The exhibits glister
beneath their shadows, stare back, refuse to blink.

The Oncology Community

Here, where lights flick on early,
a squeal of wheels is a crow's
maw bolted – every blip on the monitor
is a held breath he traps in his mouth,
daren't release, in case it's his last.

You're here again, caught at the edge
of glass, struggling to get free.
Your scales pool like mercury over
each wing, their pattern unique.
I exhale, gift my journey to you
who are too tired to flap in the breeze.

In the photo I never took

This almost-photo that I never took
has you smiling with the family
you almost had on the day you

were dashed to hospital. Nobody
looking at the photo could later say,
He did look ill. In it you can see

I'm trying to make you smile. I tell
you to remember how we nearly met
that rainy Thursday in Tunbridge Wells.

I send the photo to your phone
in the ward, know you show it
to other patients, wonder if it is you

and you exist outside those walls.
Your nurse says it's a good picture
but doesn't look like you at all.

Paddock Wood to Charing Cross

We wave each morning as though we're old friends;
you in the carriage, me walking to it, a habit started
when you mistook a sneeze for a wave, waved back.

I don't even know your name. On weekday mornings
I imagine you being Gavin or Brett, bounding down
stairs for a greedy run to the gym. By noon

you've usually changed over to Rob, sometimes Robbie
if there's a queue in a shop. It doesn't mean I like you less,
afternoons are just more mundane, especially midweek.

(I wonder when Kirk Douglas was conceived. Probably
a Monday, before nine.) When I dunk a Digestive
in my tea at three, I think of linking arms with a Simon

or a Shaun, think I'm torn between the two, or lost
somewhere in 1977. When you're not here tonight
I can't help wondering what name they'll grind

on your gravestone, black handkerchief
to my face in case I might sneeze or wave.
It would be rude not to go after all we've been through.

Presence

No one saw the hollow in the bar stool,
or the breath collapsing on the window,
or felt the shift in air as you passed –
a starched whisper hurrying to the door.

No one knew how far you walked down
Western Road, thoughts slack as rope.
We didn't know how drunk you were
at St Peter's Bridge, standing on the edge

as if looking at yourself in a long mirror.
No one heard things you said weeks before,
considered your walks, at night – alone.
We were home when you clambered railings,

searched an empty sky, its unspoken words
smoothed by wind. When you stepped off
you didn't know someone felt your small life
heat their skin, if only for a moment.

text

If that's all I have left, I'd have liked full sentences,
commas, semi-colons, Capital Letters, full stops.

What I have is, *i'm ok u ok back later.*
But you weren't back. Later. Or ever.
where r u now?

After you've died

I don't want rain storms to shake the sky,
fire engines called to drain floods,
police sirens splitting air,

or people wading through rivers
that burst their banks, or canoeing
the High Street past Waterstone's.

I don't want to open a window, watch
fireworks buzz across the cosmos, stars
shine extra brightly like some kind of sign,

or a new moon sag through clouds, its sad
face peering between branches
at the bottom of my garden.

I don't want the sun to burn so strong
it strips paint from front doors,
snakes it upwards like pencil shavings,

or beaches to be full of belly-up fish,
tails flaying in a burning heat,
flesh frying on sand.

I don't need a typhoon, a rainbow,
a wild sea locking me into land –
I need a Wednesday, a queue

in the Co-op, a girl at a till
sweeping items too quickly,
bags full of food I'll never eat.

Afterwards in ink

I fell asleep with *The North* scattered across
my bed, woke to find I'm a compass point,
ISS number slapped over my forehead,
back cover promising 32 anonymous poems

to rattle through. Front cover tells me
it's full of tangled things and texts –
I agree, battle to free myself of sheets,
stagger out of bed to light the gas.

The kettle takes an age to boil. I dream
of typefaces, the kerning of letters,
print that pins itself to a page in exactly
the right place. I think of you: hair

over your face, eyes sunk like puddles
after rainstorms, head heavy with tumours
worming their gentle path through your
brain in perfect copperplate.

After the funeral

Tonight the wind sounds like you breathing.
It's cluttered, deep-throated, clatters somewhere
in your trachea, a gentle whirring in and out
like a machine plunging up and down.
I listen a little harder each time,
to know if it's you, that you are here, even now.

I hear your steps on the stairs; wait for each one,
hear the shove of your body, the effort of it.
If the gale drops, you'll be gone,
as if snuffed out, as if even a puff of air
can carry you with it into the night –
you'll drift, one small empty body
that fits into a grave-sized hole.
Let them take the day; I have no need for it.

Package

I clinch its heart-shaped body with both hands, hands that cooked
his supper, washed his dishes, held my own mouth when we laughed
too loudly and for far too long. I forgot to tell you the postman

made me sign for this package and I looped a hooped bundle
of letters with his pen on a string, took the thing
to the front room. I didn't know something so small could change

my day, so opened the gift without ceremony, didn't expect
his dried-out soused diary to unhug itself from the envelope.
No letter from the coroner, just river-rippled A5 pages.

Living with bats

Now in July when I wake
I hear the door you left open in May
shut behind you
as if it's just remembered
you'd passed,
is tidying up, severing loose ends.

I'm listening for your tread
on the stairs,
but at the south side
of the house, under edge slats,

the only sound
is bats muttering,
flapping between barge boards.
In the dark their wings
feel their way like fingers
over Braille.

Jacket

I touch his sleeve
and it comes to life,
like it's full of swallows,

swifts, nightjars
nesting in its folds –
their pointed wings

panic-stricken, fighting
their way out. In his pocket
a clutch of warm

white eggs hatch naked fledglings,
eyes sealed, feathers not yet
sprouted. Nothing

calls to them, they're lost
in the lining, stowed inside
like children, protected.

And yet when I put on his jacket,
the pockets are empty,
      sleeves barren.

Night planting

Now you've gone, I dig the garden.
Our clay's cold as liver on a slab,
sticks to the spade. It's been raining for days.

I turn top soil, manure, compost,
fork in mulch, know you are saying,
Sharp sand, grit, hear it over and over

as worms shunt their bodies
back into earth, anchor in burrows,
disappear. I can just see to push down bulbs.

This is the Moon of Earth Mothers:
Demeter, Artemis, Danu and I plant for you
agapanthus, dahlia, harebell,

and from your book I pluck words
one-by-one, cherry-pick them: *bareroot,
heirloom, raised bed* – I learn them by heart.

Acknowledgements

Acknowledgements are due to the following magazines in which some of the poems, or versions of them, first appeared: *Agenda; Envoi; The Frogmore Papers; The High Window; Ink, Sweat and Tears; Iota; The Journal; London Grip; Magma; Mslexia; New Walk Magazine; Obsessed with Pipework; Orbis; Other Poetry; Poetry Review; The Same; Stand; Skylark Review; Under the Radar*. Some of these poems appear in the pamphlet, *The Memory of Water*, Abegail Morley, Indigo Dreams Publishing (2015).

'Before you write off your imaginary sister' won the Cinnamon Single Poem Prize 2013; 'Her Story' was commended in the Frogmore Prize 2012; 'The shed = your secret life' was commended in the *Mslexia* Poetry Competition 2013; 'Losing Elena' was commended in the York Literary Festival Competition 2014. The title poem appeared in the *With You in Mind* anthology, ed. Sarah James (2015). 'Mayday' was commissioned by The Globe Theatre as part of their *Voice and the Echo* season. Haruki Murakami quote from *Dance, Dance, Dance,* (Vintage 2002).

Thanks go to Sheila Gravels and Elizabeth O'Toole who shared their love of poetry; to Bill Greenwell who helped shape mine; and to Jane Commane for gifting these poems a lodging place.